CLIVE DAVIES

CLIVE DAVIES OBE, MA has a vast experience in primary education, covering Ofsted inspections, consultancies, headteaching and as a classroom practitioner. He has vast experience of analysing school's self-evaluations and works at supporting senior management teams in helping to construct purposeful self-evaluation procedures.

Whilst a headteacher Clive's school gained a National Curriculum award and his school was featured in the Times Educational Supplement as one of 3 recognised for its quality practice. Clive is well known nationally and internationally having worked in schools throughout England and Wales as well as Dubai, Kuwait, Saudi Arabia, Greece, Turkey, Holland, Germany and Spain.

Clive's best known publication 'Raising Standards by Setting Targets has been purchased by more than half of all primary schools in this country. Remarks like, 'You have helped to shape our thinking', and 'Your publications have made a real difference to our school' are frequently used on monitoring forms. His other publications include monitoring guidance on individual subjects as well as the nationally acclaimed, 'Chloe's Voice' recommended as a wonderful resource within the National Literacy Strategy's approach to punctuation.

ALSO BY CLIVE DAVIES

Raising Standards by Setting Targets

Achieving the Mark: Moving from Target Setting to Self Evaluation

Striding through the Stepping Stones (co author)

Chloe's Voice

The Subject Leaders Handbook (co author)

Focus Foundation Stage Progress Tracker

Focus Key Stage 1 Progress Tracker

Scrutinising Children's Work at Key Stage 2

First Published in the UK in 2007 by Focus Education (UK) Ltd.

Focus Education (UK) Ltd
Publishing
Talking Point Conference and Exhibition Centre
Huddersfield Road
Scouthead
Oldham
OL4 4AG

Focus Education (UK) Ltd Reg. No 4507968
ISBN 978-1-904469-53-7

Companies, institutions and other organisations wishing to make bu books published by Focus Education should contact their local boo Education direct:

Customer Services
Focus Education, Talking Point, Huddersfield Road, Scouthead, Oldham, O
Tel 01457 872427 Fax 01457 878205

Printed in Great Britain by The Studio (Manchester) Ltd, Swinton, Manchester.

Introduction

Using work scrutiny as a monitoring tool

- Work scrutiny is an essential part of any monitoring programme in school. It is recommended that you view it as an element of monitoring which can sit alongside other monitoring tools to help inform the bigger picture. Work scrutiny can provide very powerful evidence which helps address the recurring challenge for school leaders.

- The main focus needs to be on......

How well are pupils achieving?

Are all pupils achieving well enough?

- As with all monitoring, it is essential that you are clear about your focus before starting in order to ensure the best use of time. If used as part of an evidence trail your purpose will already have been established and the scrutiny of work will link to other types of monitoring.

Ensuring that you have a Focus

- **Decide your focus and stick to it!**

- Even those with the clearest intentions can end up being distracted from the core purpose of the scrutiny and end up focusing their attention on presentation, handwriting and marking. These are all important factors and you will have agreed school guidelines and expectations relating to them. They all need monitoring within their own right but it is important that they do not become the focus of every work scrutiny.

Know your focus

**Consider carefully what it is that you are going to focus on.
Your focus could be related to any one of the following:**

- Curricular coverage ~	- Differentiation ~	~ Pupil self-assessment ~
~ Curricular breadth ~	~ Continuity across a year group	~ Marking and feedback ~
~ Standards ~	~ Progression between year groups ~	~ Inclusion of specific groups ~
~ Progress ~	~ Range of work ~	~ Presentation ~
~ Achievement ~	~ Quality ~	~ Expectations & challenge ~
~ Underachievement ~	~ Application of basic skills ~	~ Evaluation of intervention strategies ~

Considerations

	When carrying out any work scrutiny consider the following:
Focus	Know your focus. Keep the focus tight and don't try and look at too many things at once.
Sample	Know which sample of children's work you are looking at. Consider carefully which work will give you the best evidence base to deal with your chosen issue. Consider which groups of children need to be represented in the scrutiny, e.g. random, gender specific, under-performing, SEN, least able, more able, most able, EAL learners, ethnic groups etc.
Time limit	Know how long you are allocating to complete the scrutiny and stick to it. On the whole a work scrutiny shouldn't take must longer than one hour. If it does, your focus may be too broad.

Documentation

It can be helpful to have some basic documentation to hand which can support a work scrutiny:	
Descriptors	National Curriculum level descriptors can be helpful when making judgements about standards and achievement. Use these alongside the descriptors in this book.
Planning	Planning documentation can be helpful for some work scrutinies, e.g. if you are looking at differentiation it may be helpful to compare the planning with the written outcomes.
Assessment Data	Sometimes it is helpful to know the most recent assessment outcomes for the children you are looking at to provide a context for their work.

Remember

- The main thing to remember is that you need to be evaluative. In other words, keep the following two words in your head ......

So what

- This will be essential if the work scrutiny is going to move practice forward.

- Your record of the work scrutiny needs to briefly describe what you saw and then also evaluate and make a judgement about the effectiveness of the work.

Ways of Scrutinising Written Work

There are many ways to structure a work scrutiny – you need to consider which is the most appropriate for the purpose and your context.		
Cold i.e. away from the context	Sitting alongside pupils in the classroom	Discussion with pupils using written work as starting point or prompt
With teachers, i.e. as a collaborative exercise	Looking at whole set of books	Looking at a selection of books
Looking at work on display	Looking at books from parallel classes	Tracking work of specific pupils

Standard Progress Expectation

- This book helps you identify exactly the level of attainment of each child in Years 1 and 2. To do this great care has been taken to link the P scales, the Foundation Stage profile and National Curriculum levels.

- The Key Stage 1 Scrutiny book identifies 24 stages in total. They are small, even jumps that take children from the levels identified within the Foundation Stage Profile to the National Curriculum levels. It also identifies the points at which they converge, e.g., FSP Point 9 (lower) being a lower National Curriculum Level 1b(lower).

- The Foundation Stage Profile points have been merged with P scales to help provide the Stages 1 to 11. The FS Profile is not intended to be used as a measure for progress in Key Stage 1 but by using the P scales it is possible to use the framework that has been set out in the following page. In addition, an approximate average point score (aps) has been included for the convenience of linking the progress with RAISEonline measures.

- A good guide is to accept that Stage 1 can equate to a child who is presently matching the description that is outlined for that area. For example, in writing, a child entering Year 1 at Stage 1 is likely to have been recognised at FS Profile point 1 for CLL at the end of the Reception year. In the same way a child entering Year 1 at Stage 3 in history is likely to have been recognised as being at FS Profile point 3 in KUW at the end of the reception.

- The next page identifies these points.

Standard Progress Expectation

This table identifies the 24 Stages mentioned in the previous page.
In this table FSP refers to the Foundation Stage Profile and NC refers to National Curriculum Levels.

FSP Point 1	FSP Point 2	FSP Point 3	FSP Point 4/5 (Lower)	FSP Point 4/5 (Upper)	FSP Point 6/7 (Lower)	FSP Point 6/7 (Upper)	FSP Point 8 (Lower) NC Level 1c (Lower)	
Stage 1	Stage 2	Stage 3	Stage 4	Stage 5	Stage 6	Stage 7	Stage 8	⬇
Aps 1	Aps 2	Aps 3	Aps 4	Aps 4	Aps 5	Aps 5	Aps 6	

FSP Point 8 (Upper) NC Level 1c (Secure)	FSP Point 9 (Lower) NC Level 1c (Upper)	FSP Point 9 (Upper) NC Level 1b (Secure)	National Curriculum Level 1b (Upper)	National Curriculum Level 1a (Secure)	National Curriculum Level 1a (Upper)	National Curriculum Level 2c (Secure)	National Curriculum Level 2c (Upper)	
Stage 9	Stage 10	Stage 11	Stage 12	Stage 13	Stage 14	Stage 15	Stage 16	⬇
Aps 7	Aps 8	Aps 9	Aps 10	Aps 11	Aps 12	Aps 13	Aps 14	

National Curriculum Level 2b (Secure)	National Curriculum Level 2b (Upper)	National Curriculum Level 2a (Secure)	National Curriculum Level 2a (Upper)	National Curriculum Level 3c (Secure)	National Curriculum Level 3c (Upper)	National Curriculum Level 3b (Secure)	National Curriculum Level 3b (Upper)	
Stage 17	Stage 18	Stage 19	Stage 20	Stage 21	Stage 22	Stage 23	Stage 24	
Aps 15	Aps 16	Aps 17	Aps 18	Aps 19	Aps 20	Aps 21	Aps 22	

Scrutinising Work at Key Stage One:
Writing

Writing:

Main Attributes of Writing Taking Account of the Identified Bands

Stage 1: Children Identified at FSP Point 1 should show the following attributes: APS 1	Stage 2: Children Identified at FSP Point 2 should show the following attributes: APS 2
• Is happy to make up, draw and talk about stories associated with the drawings; • Is selective about the range of drawing equipment used; • Recognises that drawing and writing are different; • Makes marks, but does not always ascribe meaning to the marks, although there is a general awareness of the writing purpose.	• Is beginning to form recognisable letters; • Assigns a message to own symbols, drawing or scribbles; • Knows that writing communicates meaning; • Is able to tell an adult what to write; • Recognises own name in print.

Writing:

Main Attributes of Writing Taking Account of the Identified Bands

Stage 3: Children Identified at FSP Point 3 should show the following attributes: APS 3	Stage 4: Children Identified at FSP Point 4/5 Lower should show the following attributes: APS 4
• Experiments with upper and lower case; • Shows an awareness of directionality; • Can point to where print begins; • Sometimes mixes up letters, numbers and invented letter shapes; • Uses left to right and top to bottom conventions of print.	• Is beginning to form recognisable letters showing some control over size, shape and orientation; • Has established an effective pencil grip.

Writing:

Main Attributes of Writing Taking Account of the Identified Bands

Stage 5: Children Identified at FSP Point 4/5 Upper should show the following attributes: APS 4+	Stage 6: Children Identified at FSP Point 6/7 Lower should show the following attributes: APS 5
• Writes at least first name, as well some other words; • Sometimes writes key words that are important to them; • Can spell first name with correct use of capitalisation; • Begins to write some familiar high frequency words correctly, e.g. mum, dad.	• Writes lists, cards and instructions; • Is able to use word banks, charts, signs and sentence starters to help to structure their writing; • Is beginning to copy the layout of some text forms, e.g. letters and lists; • Adds labels and captions to pictures.

Writing:

Main Attributes of Writing Taking Account of the Identified Bands

Stage 7: Children Identified at FSP Point 6/7 Upper should show the following attributes: APS 5+	Stage 8: Children Identified at 1c Lower (FSP Point 8 Lower) should show the following attributes: APS 6
• Can write each letter in response to its sound; • The first letter of a word is correctly used; • The last letter of a word is often used; • Is beginning to use other dominant phonemes in words; • Writing gives the reader a good idea of the content or main purpose.	• Can record in writing something they have done; • Can retell or make up a story using puppets or pictures to help; • Makes sure that all letters are easy for people to read; • Writes first name and surname correctly using capital letters, where needed; • Spells correctly familiar CVC words (e.g., cat, dog).

Writing:

Main Attributes of Writing Taking Account of the Identified Bands

Stage 9: Children Identified at 1c Secure (FSP Point 8 Upper) should show the following attributes: **APS 7**	Stage 10: Children Identified at 1c Upper (FSP Point 9 Lower) should show the following attributes: **APS 8**
• Sentences contains specific words or phrases that are to do with the subject being written about; • Says out aloud what they want to write before writing it; • With help, is able to read writing back to someone; • Knows that a full stop is used to finish sentences; • Attempts to spell an unfamiliar word using a phonic strategy.	• Writes a sentence about something that has happened in the past; • Anyone reading the writing can make sense of it; • Full stops are used in the correct place; • Can talk about at least two things that have happenedat home.

Writing:

Main Attributes of Writing Taking Account of the Identified Bands

Stage 11: Children Identified at 1b Secure (FSP Point 9 Upper) should show the following attributes: APS 9	Stage 12: Children Identified at 1b Upper should show the following attributes: APS 10
• Writing is easy to follow and makes sense; • Can write simple questions about something they want to find out about; • Uses words and phrases to help build up ideas about a character; • Makes sure that all letters are formed correctly and are about the same size.	• Careful thought has been given to the words used so that the writing makes sense; • Each piece of writing has at least one good idea; • Rehearses what is written by saying sentence out aloud to check that they make sense; • Remembers to use finger spaces between words; • Uses capital letters to start sentences.

Writing:

Main Attributes of Writing Taking Account of the Identified Bands

Stage 13: Children Identified at 1a Secure should show the following attributes: APS 11	Stage 14: Children Identified at 1a Upper should show the following attributes: APS 12
• Stories have one or more characters and setting; • Reads writing aloud to check it makes sense; • Writes out simple instructions in the correct order; • Makes sure that all letters are always the right way round.	• Makes sentences longer and can join two ideas together; • Writing contains more than one idea and more than one character; • Starts of my stories are interesting; • Uses capital letters as well as full stops, including 'I'; • Does not to mix up capital letters and small letters.

Writing:

Main Attributes of Writing Taking Account of the Identified Bands

Stage 15: Children Identified at 2c Secure should show the following attributes: APS 13	Stage 16: Children Identified at 2c Upper should show the following attributes: APS 14
• Uses words like 'then' to join two ideas together in the correct order; • Write more than one thing about each idea; • People can make sense of writing without needing to have it explained; • Sounds out spelling of words if not sure.	• Changes the way sentences start; • Make sentences longer and uses words other than 'and' and 'then' to join ideas together; • Has a good idea about who the writing is aimed at; • Uses new words that haven't been used before in stories and writing; • Does not mix up capital and small case letters; • Knows which letters are tall and which ones fall below the line.

Writing:

Main Attributes of Writing Taking Account of the Identified Bands

Stage 17: Children Identified at 2b Secure should show the following attributes: APS 15	Stage 18: Children Identified at 2b Upper should show the following attributes: APS 16
• Uses at least one describing word in each sentence; • Sentences include time connectives, such as then, after, before or meanwhile; • Ideas follow one another in a sequence that makes sense; • Can set out a letter properly; • Capital letters are used for the names of people and places; • Uses question marks when needed.	• The writing has something of interest in it helping people to enjoy reading it; • Descriptions are very clear so that people can recognise what is meant even when things are not named; • When writing, uses some of the phrases and words that they come across in reading; • Makes an effort to use words like, 'suddenly' or 'amazingly', so that writing grip the reader's interest; • Attempts to use commas in the correct place.

Writing:

Main Attributes of Writing Taking Account of the Identified Bands

Stage 19: Children Identified at 2a Secure should show the following attributes: APS 17	Stage 20: Children Identified at 2a Upper should show the following attributes: APS 18
• Stories have interesting endings that have been carefully thought about; • The beginnings of stories are exciting and interesting and make people want to read more; • Has thought about the differences between story writing and other types of writing; • Is consistent in using the first or third person; • Uses exclamation marks, if they are needed.	• Uses more interesting connectives other than 'and' and 'but' to join my sentences; • Tries to make sure that the same words are not used all the time; • Stories are organised so that there is a clear beginning, middle and ending; • Keeps writing interesting throughout and is not tempted to look at quick ways to finish it; • Checks that capital letters, commas and question marks are used when needed and begins to use speech marks; • Uses a dictionary appropriately to check spellings of words.

Writing:

Main Attributes of Writing Taking Account of the Identified Bands

Stage 21: Children Identified at 3c Secure should show the following attributes: APS 19	Stage 22: Children Identified at 3c Upper should show the following attributes: APS 20
• Uses specific nouns when needed, e.g. 'terrier' instead of 'dog'; • Writes compound, as well as simple, sentences; • The middle part of stories have at least two good ideas; • Uses different words that have not been used before in writing; • Takes time to describe characters and events within stories rather than move from one event to another; • Can edit writing according to who is likely to read it, adding or removing parts as necessary; • Uses commas when writing a list.	• All sentences begin in a range of interesting ways; • Uses adjectives and adverbs with confidence and attempts to think of different ones to use in different situations; • Consistently uses the correct first and third person when writing; • Gives careful thought to the planning of writing and re-reads it as a matter of course; • Ensures that descriptions have just enough detail to help the reader gain a better understanding about the way the story is unfolding; • Writes legibly with a joined hand, maintaining consistency in size and spacing; • Checks punctuation and uses speech marks and apostrophes accurately; • Applies known rules and conventions when trying to spell unknown words.

Writing:

Main Attributes of Writing Taking Account of the Identified Bands

Stage 23: Children Identified at 3b Secure should show the following attributes:

APS 21

- Uses generalisations such as 'always' or 'never' when expressing opinion;

- Consistently uses correct tenses when writing;

- Writing includes clear images related to the subject that is being written about;

- When needed, writing will contain aspects of humour or suspense;

- Begins to consider different styles of handwriting for different purposes, e.g., note-taking;

- Uses apostrophes for possession accurately. e.g., dad's, dads';

- Spells correctly words containing common prefixes and suffixes, e.g., un-, dis-, -ly, -ful;

- Uses apostrophes, when needed, to show that a letter/s has been omitted.

Writing:

Main Attributes of Writing Taking Account of the Identified Bands

Stage 24: Children Identified at 3b Upper should show the following attributes: APS 22

- Uses a range of adjectives and adverbs to make descriptions more interesting;

- Sentences are full of detail and include interesting words and phrases;

- Attempts to use words that haven't been used before when describing events, characters and feelings;

- Uses powerful verbs to show character or add impact;

- Varies sentences, adding phrases to make the meaning more precise;

- Chooses the most appropriate style of writing to suit the needs of the situations. That is, poems, lists, letters, report, etc.;

- Makes sure writing will not jump from one idea to another too often;

- Writing will sometimes contain humour; and descriptions of events and characters can be done in a variety of ways and sometimes include humour;

- Uses imagination when describing places and events in stories;

- Description of characters include feelings and emotions, when it is needed;

- Non-fiction writing is able to interest, instruct, persuade or amuse the reader;

- Uses commas to separate phrases or clauses within sentences.

Scrutinising Work at Key Stage One:
Reading

Reading:

Main Attributes of Reading, Taking Account of the Identified Bands

Stage 1: Children Identified at FSP Point 1 should show the following attributes: APS 1	Stage 2: Children Identified at FSP Point 2 should show the following attributes: APS 2
• Takes part in book sharing activities, listening to and joining in with stories, poems and rhymes; • Enjoys stories and has favourite books; • Chooses to look at books independently when in the book area showing a particular interest in illustrations in books; • Handles books appropriately, turning pages appropriately and holding it the correct way up.	• Understands the difference between print and illustration; • Can distinguish between the sound made by different phonemes and begins to notice when words have the same beginning sound; • Is aware that signs and symbols in the environment carry meaning; • Has observed print being used for many purposes, e.g., register, etc.; • Shows an awareness of words which rhyme.

Reading:

Main Attributes of Reading, Taking Account of the Identified Bands

Stage 3: Children Identified at FSP Point 3 should show the following attributes: APS 3	Stage 4: Children Identified at FSP Point 4/5 Lower should show the following attributes: APS 4
• Recognises some familiar words in the environment, such as McDonalds, Tesco, etc.; • Is able to talk about familiar texts showing curiosity about the text at a simple level; • Begins to recognise, name and sound some letters of personal significance, such as own name in familiar contexts, e.g., coat peg, name card, etc.; • With support, recognises some key words within the classroom captions and labels, e.g., milk, door, book, etc.	• Uses correct 'directionality' when reading independently; • When discussing a familiar story recognises that most stories have a main character and identifies the main characters; • Can talk to an adult about common features of a story, e.g., good and bad characters; • When discussing a familiar story identifies the main sequence of events.

Reading:

Main Attributes of Reading, Taking Account of the Identified Bands

Stage 5: Children Identified at FSP Point 4/5 Upper should show the following attributes: **APS 4+**	Stage 6: Children Identified at FSP Point 6/7 Lower should show the following attributes: **APS 5**
• Turns pages of a book one at a time and shows where the beginning and end of a book is; • Follows text using finger, starting at the top left hand side and with the first line; • Uses pictorial cues when sharing a book or 'reading'; • Is aware of the sequence in a familiar story; • Can talk to an adult about the main events in a story and can say how a story starts and ends; • Recalls openings of familiar stories within their own imaginative play.	• Reads at least 20 words common words in a range of contexts; • Uses a range of cues, including knowledge of a story or context, what makes sense grammatically and word/letter recognition to help read words; • Is able to predict words, symbols, signs or phases in familiar text; • Retells the main points or events of a simple narrative in correct sequence, using linking language; • Makes use of language patterns such as 'Run, run , as fast as you can' are remembered and used.

Reading:

Main Attributes of Reading, Taking Account of the Identified Bands

Stage 7: **Children Identified at FSP Point 6/7 Upper should show the following attributes:**

APS 5+

- Uses familiarity with stories to help read simple sentences;

- Uses knowledge of key words to help read full sentences;

- Makes good use of a range of cues including familiarity, pictures and recognition of individual words to help read simple sentences;

- Can retell a simple narrative putting the main events in correct sequence;

- Uses the language specific to the story, including repetitive phrases;

- Uses story language when telling a story;

- Begins to apply knowledge of letter sounds to attempt to read words within familiar texts.

Reading:

Main Attributes of Reading, Taking Account of the Identified Bands

Stage 8: Children Identified at 1c Lower (FSP Point 8 Lower) should show the following attributes: **APS 6**	Stage 9: Children Identified at 1c Secure (FSP Point 8 Upper) should show the following attributes: **APS 7**
• Is able to talk about the text they like and dislike; • Points to specific known words as they read; • Recognises initial letter sounds in unfamiliar words; • Can follow simple texts when it is read to them.	• Can join in with parts of familiar text, especially repeated text or rhymes; • Can listen attentively to story; • Can use picture clues to help read simple text.

Reading:

Main Attributes of Reading, Taking Account of the Identified Bands

Stage 10: Children Identified at 1c Upper (FSP Point 9 Lower) should show the following attributes: APS 8	Stage 11: Children Identified at 1b Secure (FSP Point 9 Upper) should show the following attributes: APS 9
• Can read a range of familiar words; • Can recognise initial and final letter sounds in unfamiliar words; • Uses knowledge of letters/ sounds to establish meaning.	• Responds to events and ideas in nonfiction, when asked; • Can show understanding of the main ideas and events in a story; • Can guess at immediate events.

Reading:

Main Attributes of Reading, Taking Account of the Identified Bands

Stage 12: Children Identified at 1b Upper should show the following attributes: **APS 10**	Stage 13: Children Identified at 1a Secure should show the following attributes: **APS 11**
• Sounds out CVC words without prompt; • Reads a range of high frequency words (first level) without prompt; • Expresses likes and dislikes about a wide range of texts; • Able to predict what happens next in familiar texts; • Can read aloud with support.	• Can establish meaning when reading aloud; • Can read familiar signs and labels; • Can recognise phonetically regular words; • Is willing to make an attempts at unknown words using knowledge of letters and sounds; • Can make simple deductions with help and prompt from adults.

Reading:

Main Attributes of Reading, Taking Account of the Identified Bands

Stage 14: Children Identified at 1a Upper should show the following attributes: **APS 12**	Stage 15: Children Identified at 2c Secure should show the following attributes: **APS 13**
• Reads more than 90% of a passage independently (that is from an appropriate selection of books for this stage of reading); • Is aware of mistakes that have been made in their reading; • Is using phonics to help decode unknown words; • Re-reads a passage in an attempt to clarify meaning.	• Is able to re-tell the main events or give further information about a character in the text; • Is able to comment on the most obvious features in the text with the help of an adult; • The reading tends to be word by word; • Still relies heavily on illustrations; • Is beginning to use more than one strategy for decoding; • Has a good understanding about the way informational text is organised; • Is beginning to have a grasp of plot.

Reading:

Main Attributes of Reading, Taking Account of the Identified Bands

Stage 16: Children Identified at 2c Upper should show the following attributes: **APS 14**	Stage 17: Children Identified at 2b Secure should show the following attributes: **APS 15**
• Reading is almost entirely accurate (from a given range of text); • Is more aware of sentence construction and uses full stops to aid expression; • The reading is normally well paced especially in parts of the texts; • Is able to read ahead; • Extends the range of strategies used to decode unfamiliar texts; • Sometimes notices when the reading does not make sense.	• Usually self-corrects or attempts to use a strategy to work out error; • Using graphic clues as an additional aid to help with reading; • Understands and comments on plot, setting and characters in familiar and unfamiliar texts; • Understands and comments on how information is presented in fiction, nonfiction and poetry; • Comments on the setting; • Re-telling of the story refers to most, if not all, the main characters; • Can distinguish between fact and opinion.

Reading:

Main Attributes of Reading, Taking Account of the Identified Bands

Stage 18: Children Identified at 2b Upper should show the following attributes: **APS 16**	Stage 19: Children Identified at 2a Secure should show the following attributes: **APS 17**
• Reading is accurate. Can read simple, unfamiliar text accurately. • Is able to use a wide range of decoding skills to tackle unfamiliar words; • Is able to read ahead to confirm meaning; • Can enhance meaning through expression and intonation; • Identifies and comments on main characters in stories and how they relate to one another.	• Expresses own opinion about events and actions in text; • Sometimes notices when the reading does not make sense and takes appropriate action; • Self-corrects, looks backwards and forwards in the text and searches for meaning; • Identifies and comments on the main characters; • Comments on how characters relate to one another; • Can comment on opinion about alternative things that might have happened and can make predictions; • Begins to comment about the way the writing is presented; • Can use knowledge of the alphabet to locate information in dictionaries.

Reading:

Main Attributes of Reading, Taking Account of the Identified Bands

Stage 20: Children Identified at 2a Upper should show the following attributes: APS 18	Stage 21: Children Identified at 3c Secure should show the following attributes: APS 19
• Can show understanding of the main points of the text and re-tell the story; • Can read independently, using a range of reading strategies appropriately to establish meaning; • Can express reading preferences – both by naming authors and by talking about types of stories; • Can make sensible predictions about what is likely to happen in the story and to different characters; • Know how suspense is built up in a story, including the development of the plot.	• Can prepare a reading that conveys humour; • Can recognise similarities in the plot or characters within different stories; • Can read poetry using intonation and expression and handle humour appropriately, when needed; • Can extract information from non-fiction texts, using contents, index, chapters, headings and glossary appropriately; • Can recognise the main differences between fiction and non-fiction text.

Reading:

Main Attributes of Reading, Taking Account of the Identified Bands

Stage 22: Children Identified at 3c Upper should show the following attributes: APS 20	Stage 23: Children Identified at 3b Secure should show the following attributes: APS 21
• Can read a range of texts fluently and accurately; • Can compare different versions of the same myth and legend; • Can identify language within the text that is different from that in everyday use; • Can dramatise and perform a story for others, using a narrator, if necessary; • Can use appropriate voices for characters and adapt a story telling voice when needed.	• Can compare how different news is presented in different formats; • Can skim materials and note down different views and arguments; • Can distinguish between fact and opinion; • Can pause appropriately in response to punctuation and/or meaning; • Can justify predications they make by referring to the story; • Considers different formats and approaches to book reviews.

Reading:

Main Attributes of Reading, Taking Account of the Identified Bands

Stage 24: **Children Identified at 3b Upper should show the following attributes:**

APS 22

- Can begin to find meaning beyond the literal, for example, how impressions of people are conveyed, through choice of detail and language;

- Can respond to the tension in a story;

- Can read ahead to determine direction and meaning in a story;

- Investigates what is known about the historical setting and events and their importance to the story;

- Uses inference and deduction to work out what characters are like from evidence in the text;

- Explores figurative language and how it conveys meaning succinctly;

- Is able to explore the relationship between a poet and the subject of a poem;

- Can identify how a writer sets out to persuade;

- Can skim materials to gain an overview or overall impression;

- Can devise questions and scan materials to locate information and answers.

Scrutinising Work at Key Stage One:
Mathematics

Mathematics:

Main Attributes of Mathematics, Taking Account of the Identified Bands

Stage 1: Children Identified at FSP Point 1 should show the following attributes: APS 1	Stage 2: Children Identified at FSP Point 2 should show the following attributes: APS 2
• Recites some number rhymes and songs. Joins in rote counting; • Joins in rhymes and songs involving subtraction such as 'Five Currant Buns'; • In practical contexts begins to use some of the vocabulary involved in subtraction, e.g., 'one less'; • Attempts to use fingers, pictures and objects to accompany rhymes and songs; • Enjoys creating pictures from shapes; • Makes arrangements with blocks and other objects.	• Counts by rote to at least 3; • Can count reliably up to 3 objects using 1 to 1 correspondence; • Can count or take up to 3 objects from a larger set; • Can compare groups of objects with large differences, being able to identify which has more/ less; • Matches simple shapes with support; • Can recognise similar shapes of different sizes; • Sorts objects according to features such as size and colour.

Mathematics:

Main Attributes of Mathematics, Taking Account of the Identified Bands

Stage 3: Children Identified at FSP Point 3 should show the following attributes: APS 3	Stage 4: Children Identified at FSP Point 4/5 Lower should show the following attributes: APS 4
• Can count out or take up to 6 objects from a larger set; • In practical situations with everyday objects is able to find one less. For example, 'There are 3 speckled frogs on a log, one jumps in the pond. So how many are there now?'; • Can subtract one from a group or set of objects up to 5 and count how many left; • Is beginning to talk about the features of shapes using simple vocabulary such as flat/ pointy.	• Uses the number names to 10 in order in familiar contexts such as number rhymes/ counting games; • Has begun to recognise none and zero in stories/ rhymes/ counting games; • Recognises numbers of personal significance, such as 3 or 4; • Can add two groups of objects accurately by combining them and counting all the objects for totals of up to 10; • Is able to relate the language used to known shapes such as square, circle, triangle; • Can copy and continue a simple pattern.

Mathematics:

Main Attributes of Mathematics, Taking Account of the Identified Bands

Stage 5: Children Identified at FSP Point 4/5 Upper should show the following attributes: APS 4+	Stage 6: Children Identified at FSP Point 6/7 Lower should show the following attributes: APS 5
• Can recite the numbers in order from zero to at least ten and back again; • Can recognise all numbers between 1 and 9. Is beginning to copy these numbers from the environment, e.g., door numbers, labels, etc.; • Using everyday objects says how many objects are left when some are eaten, taken away or hidden by counting them, taking some away and then counting those that are left; • Can separate a given number of objects into two groups and say how many are in each group; • Responds to instructions by placing objects appropriately, in/out; under/over; in front/ behind; next to/ away from.	• Can count or take away up to 10 objects away from a larger set; • Uses their knowledge of number order to say which number comes next for numbers to ten; • In practical activities and discussion begins to use vocabulary relating to subtraction such as less; take away; and how many left; • Can compare objects by size, using terms bigger; longer; shorter; • Has begun to recognise and name common, regular 2D shapes – such as circle; triangle; square and oblong and can select the appropriate shape when asked; • Describes and explores the properties of shapes and can determine which shapes can slide or roll.

Mathematics:

Main Attributes of Mathematics, Taking Account of the Identified Bands

Stage 7: Children Identified at FSP Point 6/7 Upper should show the following attributes:

APS 5+

- Can recognise the numbers zero to ten;

- Can compare two numbers between zero and 10, saying which is the larger or smaller;

- Can order written numbers up to 10;

- Can add one more or take away one from a group or set of up to 10 objects and count how many altogether;

- Can use their knowledge of number order to find the number that is one more or one less than a given number from 1 to 10;

- Understands and uses language such as heavy/ light; and full/ empty;

- Can compare two masses saying which is heavier or lighter;

- Uses terms such as more or less when comparing capacity.

Mathematics:

Main Attributes of Mathematics, Taking Account of the Identified Bands

Stage 8: Children Identified at 1c Lower (FSP Point 8 Lower) should show the following attributes: **APS 6**	Stage 9: Children Identified at 1c Secure (FSP Point 8 Upper) should show the following attributes: **APS 7**
• Counts object to and matches numbers to10; • Read and writes all numbers to 10; (although reversals may be evident); • Can correct reversals in numbers when asked to check them out; • Can estimate to 10; • Uses vocabulary such as: too many; more estimate, none, nought. • Can order numbers to at least 10; • Ordering sequence can include 0.	• Adds one more and counts; • Can add two sets of objects to 10; • Uses vocabulary such as: plus; 'how many more'; • Records with number sentences using the term 'and makes'; • Can take one away and works out how many are left; • Can remove a smaller number of objects from a larger one and work out how many are left; • Uses vocabulary such as: fewer; • Can talk about and use the numbers set out in the previous columns within the context of number stories, as well as home ands school life; • Can continue a repeating pattern.

Mathematics:

Main Attributes of Mathematics, Taking Account of the Identified Bands

Stage 10: Children Identified at 1c Upper (FSP Point 9 Lower) should show the following attributes: APS 8	Stage 11: Children Identified at 1b Secure (FSP Point 9 Upper) should show the following attributes: APS 9
• Counts object beyond 10; • Matches numbers to 10; • Read and writes all numbers to 10; • Can order numbers to at least 10, including zero; • Adds one more and counts to 10; • Can record orally or pictorially; • Can record using number sentences; • Can take one away and works out how many are left (up to 10); • Can record orally or pictorially; • Can recognise a repeating pattern.	• Can estimate to 10; • Uses vocabulary such as: too many; more; estimate; none; • Can order numbers beyond 10 with pictorial support; • Uses vocabulary, such as: between, before, after, next; • Can add two or three sets to 10; • Uses vocabulary such as: plus, how many more and altogether; • Can record using number sentences; • Uses vocabulary such as: less, fewer, take away; • Can talk about and use the numbers set out in the previous columns within the context of number stories, as well as home ands school life; • Can make a repeating pattern; • Counts the number of objects involved in a repeating pattern.

Mathematics:

Main Attributes of Mathematics, Taking Account of the Identified Bands

Stage 12: Children Identified at 1b Upper should show the following attributes: APS 10	Stage 13: Children Identified at 1a Secure should show the following attributes: APS 11
• Counts sets of objects with consistent accuracy well beyond 10; • When writing numbers larger than 10 will sometimes make reversals of the two digits but recognises inaccuracy when this is pointed out; • Can find a missing number in a simple sequence that increases by one; • Begins to use the symbol +; • Begins to use the symbol -; • Begins to understand and use the symbol =; • Demonstrates confidence in working with numbers up to 30, with the aid of mathematical equipment.	• Is aware of the pattern that exists when writing numbers beyond 10; • Can order numbers to about 30; • Knows how much to add to a given number to make a larger number (up to about 20); • Demonstrates the use of recall of low numbers rather than relying on counting; • Knows how much to take away from a given number to leave a smaller number (up to about 20); • Uses vocabulary such as, minus; • Is more confident working with higher numbers for the purpose of addition rather than subtraction; • When presented with written subtractions will often make 'smaller from larger' unit error unless using apparatus or a number line.

Mathematics:

Main Attributes of Mathematics, Taking Account of the Identified Bands

Stage 14: **Children Identified at 1a Upper should show the following attributes:** APS 12	Stage 15: **Children Identified at 2c Secure should show the following attributes:** APS 13
• Can read numbers up to 100; • Can order numbers to at least 100; • Uses mental recall to add two numbers to 10; • Uses and responds to the symbols + and =; • Uses mental recall to 10, but not confidently as with addition; • Subtraction is typically carried out by counting back on a number line or removing objects; • Uses and responds to symbols – and =; • Recognises and uses halves in a practical context;	• May be able to write numbers to 100 but is less secure; • May continue to make some errors with higher two-digit numbers; • Uses a pattern to support ordering of numbers to 100; • Can continue a number sequence with lower numbers; • Adds two lower two-digit numbers by counting on using a number line or objects; • When presented with written subtractions will often make 'smaller from larger' unit error unless using apparatus or a number line; • Can select addition or subtraction to solve problems if it is presented in a familiar context and the language used is not confusing; • Can recognise and use quarters in a practical context, but usually requires help.

Mathematics:

Main Attributes of Mathematics, Taking Account of the Identified Bands

Stage 16: Children Identified at 2c Upper should show the following attributes: APS 14	Stage 17: Children Identified at 2b Secure should show the following attributes: APS 15
• Can read and write numbers to 100; • Sometimes unsure of the correct digit order when writing a few (higher) numbers; • Can use a number line or a pattern to count; • Can partition a two-digit number into tens and units; • Begins to use mental recall of number bonds within 10 to add two-digit numbers; • Begins to apply knowledge of number bonds within 10 to s subtract one-digit number from a two-digit number; • Can select addition or subtraction to solve problems; • Can recognise and show half and quarter of a familiar shape; • May make mistakes when doing so with triangles.	• Can count high numbers of objects in twos, fives or tens; • Can recognise and use simple number sequences (twos, threes, fours, fives and tens); • Can recognise odd and even numbers; • Can order numbers and familiar measures, for example, money (within 100) starting with the largest or the smallest; • Begins to apply understanding of two-digit numbers as tens and units to addition of two-digit numbers; • Can use apparatus or number line/grid to subtract a two-digit number form a larger two-digit number; • Will be more confident with smaller numbers below 30; • Will naturally be more confident with addition than subtraction; • Can find half or a quarter of numbers to 20 that are multiple of two or four respectively.

Mathematics:

Main Attributes of Mathematics, Taking Account of the Identified Bands

Stage 18: Children Identified at 2b Upper should show the following attributes: APS 16	Stage 19: Children Identified at 2a Secure should show the following attributes: APS 17
• Can count and write numbers to 1000; although may require some support with the written numbers; • Has better understanding of place value with tens and units; • Able to discuss numbers in terms of hundreds, tens and units; • Uses mental recall of number bonds within 10 to add two-digit numbers; • Is more confident in using number bonds when subtracting; • Recognises and uses the x (multiplication) symbol; • Can find half of numbers to 20 and some higher numbers.	• Able children may demonstrate facility with negative numbers in an abstract context to -5; • Can add two two-digit numbers that require carry over from units to tens; • Can recite the 2x and 10x table; • Starts to use some recall of some number facts to solve problems in relation to multiplication; • Can find a quarter of multiples of four to 12 or 16; • Can solve simple multiplication and sharing problems. Starts to show an organised and methodical approach to solving problems.

Mathematics:

Main Attributes of Mathematics, Taking Account of the Identified Bands

Stage 20: Children Identified at 2a Upper should show the following attributes: APS 18	Stage 21: Children Identified at 3c Secure should show the following attributes: APS 19
• Can count, read and write numbers to 1000; • Can discuss numbers in terms of hundreds, tens and units; • Can round-up two-digit numbers to the nearest 10; • More secure in solving two-step problems; • Uses mental recall of number bonds to 20; • Doubles and halves numbers with confidence; • Can recognise and use multiplication and division symbols; • Still at the stage of demonstrating a more secure understanding of multiplication than division; • Very confident in applying the 2x and 10x tables.	• Can round-up three-digit numbers to the nearest 100; • Recognises negative numbers as being below zero; • Can use negative numbers to measure minus degrees in the temperature scale; • Uses mental strategies or sets out a computation to add/subtract two-digit numbers; • Uses informal methods to solve computational problems; • Still is more secure in addition rather than subtraction; • Becomes more accurate in solving subtraction problems; • Can use a calculator to solve problems that involve four-digit numbers; • Has knowledge of 5x table and is gaining in familiarity with the 3x, 4x tables.

Mathematics:

Main Attributes of Mathematics, Taking Account of the Identified Bands

Stage 22: Children Identified at 3c Upper should show the following attributes: APS 20	Stage 23: Children Identified at 3b Secure should show the following attributes: APS 21
• Consistently counts and writes numbers in 1000s; • Uses understanding of place value to approximate numbers to nearest 10 or 100 when working with three-digit numbers; • Knows addition and subtraction facts to 20; • Can apply this knowledge to work out number facts that cannot be recalled; • Uses understanding of number relationships as part of mental strategies; • Can use mental recall of 2x, 5x and 10x table; • Have knowledge of 3x and 4x tables; • Can recognise multiplication and division problems and copes sensibly with remainders; • Can apply knowledge of times table to multiplication problems;	• Starts to use decimal notation as a proportion of a unit and uses this within the context of money; • Can recognise negative numbers in the context of temperature, money and calculator display; • Recognises and uses simple fractions, within an appropriate context; • Can add and subtract two and three-digit numbers when there is carry over or decomposition in one column; • Has a more secure understanding of addition and subtraction and the relationship between them; • Can add or subtract small negative numbers using a number line; • More able children are better at using mental methods to calculate answers; • Understands multiplication as 'lots of' and repeated addition; • Understands division as sharing and begins to understand as repeated subtraction; • More able can apply the same principles to division problems; • It is quite normal for inefficient methods to be selected at this stage.

Mathematics:

Main Attributes of Mathematics, Taking Account of the Identified Bands

Stage 24: Children Identified at 3b Upper should show the following attributes:

APS 22

- Can use knowledge and understanding of place value to read and write numbers in ten thousands and hundred thousands;

- Understands relationships between fractions, for example, 2 quarters is the same as one half which is the same as four eighths, etc.;

- Starts to understand the value of numbers to the right of the decimal point;

- Begin s to relate vulgar and decimal fractions, for example, ½ = 0.5;

- Can add or subtract simple fractions and decimals to one place;

- Can select and apply efficient mental and written strategies;

- Can use these confidently with numbers to thousands;

- Developing skills in operating negative numbers;

- Increasing range of mental strategies;

- Has secure recall of 2x, 3x, 4x, 5x and 10x tables;

- Has developing knowledge of other table facts to 10;

- Uses doubling of known tables to help understand and know the value of far higher tables;

- Can identify addition and subtraction relationships in patterns or sequences of number;

- Can describe relationship in words using appropriate mathematical vocabulary.

Scrutinising Work at Key Stage One:
ICT

ICT: Main Attributes of ICT, Taking Account of the Identified Bands

Stage 1: Children Identified at FSP Point 1 should show the following attributes:	Stage 2: Children Identified at FSP Point 2 should show the following attributes:
• Is aware of the technology in everyday use, e.g., washing machines, mobile phones.	• Knows how to operate simple equipment, e.g., tape recorder, using the mouse on a computer, switching on and off a programmable toy.
Stage 3: Children Identified at FSP Point 3 should show the following attributes:	**Stage 4: Children Identified at FSP Point 4/5 Lower should show the following attributes:**
• Has an awareness of activities that can only be carried out on computers, electronic devices, etc.	• Can role play a telephone conversation; • Is aware of everyday household equipment and what they do, e.g., washing machine; television; CD player; microwave; camera and radio.

ICT: Main Attributes of ICT, Taking Account of the Identified Bands

Stage 5: Children Identified at FSP Point 4/5 Upper should show the following attributes:	Stage 6: Children Identified at FSP Point 6/7 Lower should show the following attributes:
• Can explore how things work by dismantling simple and safe objects, such as, torches and clocks; • Begins to understand how technology is used in everyday life, e.g., knows that bar code records price of items in shops.	• Demonstrates good skills in controlling a programmable toy; • Controls a floor robot to make it go forwards and backwards; • Can begin to estimate the amount of movement made by giving different instructions.

ICT: Main Attributes of ICT, Taking Account of the Identified Bands

Stage 7: Children Identified at FSP Point 6/7 Upper should show the following attributes:	Stage 8: Children Identified at 1c Lower (FSP Point 8 Lower) should show the following attributes:
• Can use icons to work through a range of computer software, including simple data handling packages; • Double clicks on an icon to start a program; • Can identify the main parts of a computer, such as, monitor; screen; keyboard and mouse; • Understands basic computer terms, such as, click; print; save and program.	• Can use the delete and backspace functions on the keyboard; • Can use a simple painting program to create a picture; • Knows that the digital camera can be used to help create pictures on the compute; • Can take very effective pictures using a camera and know what to do to improve it.

ICT: Main Attributes of ICT, Taking Account of the Identified Bands

Stage 9: Children Identified at 1c Secure (FSP Point 8 Upper) should show the following attributes:	Stage 10: Children Identified at 1c Upper (FSP Point 9 Lower) should show the following attributes:
• Is able to open a program by clicking on the appropriate icon on the desktop and can close down software; • Is able to select an icon, drag it and drop it into the correct place; • Is confident in using the space bar; • Is able to form a simple sentence on the screen, making use of a given word bank.	• Is able to save work to a personal folder; • Is able to use a mouse to move and place items accurately onto a screen; • Can use the shift key to produce capital letters; • Can use pictograms to answer simple questions.

ICT: Main Attributes of ICT, Taking Account of the Identified Bands

Stage 11: Children Identified at 1b Secure (FSP Point 9 Upper) should show the following attributes:	Stage 12: Children Identified at 1b Upper should show the following attributes:
• Is able to print out work without help; • Is able to sort out data and present it as a pictogram; • Is able to make independent choices about where text and pictures are placed; • Can describe and identify objects using key words; • Knows that it is easier to understand data that is represented graphically rather than in text.	• Is able to move a floor robot forwards and backwards to a number of specific units; • Is able to work out a sequence of instructions to give to a floor robot; • Is able to use tools like colour fill and brushes in a painting package; • Is able to use motifs from the clip art to add things to a scene created.

ICT: Main Attributes of ICT, Taking Account of the Identified Bands

Stage 13: Children Identified at 1a Secure should show the following attributes:	Stage 14: Children Identified at 1a Upper should show the following attributes:
• Is able to log on to the network using the user name; • Can record a message on a tape recorder; • Can assemble error-free text with independence; • Is able to use ICT skills to classify information and present findings in different ways.	• Can save work to own folder using the instruction SAVE AS; • Can use the return key to insert line breaks, and make lists, where appropriate; • Knows the difference between a contents page and CD ROM menus; • Knows the terms upper and lower case; • Can use capital letters or bold text to highlight or emphasis words in text; • Knows where to locate the question mark on a keyboard.

ICT: Main Attributes of ICT, Taking Account of the Identified Bands

Stage 15: Children Identified at 2c Secure should show the following attributes:	Stage 16: Children Identified at 2c Upper should show the following attributes:
• Is able to use buttons to navigate a CD ROM; • Uses menus to locate information; • Uses index to locate information; • Is able to use hyperlinks or hot links to locate information.	• Is able to delete and insert text; • Can use the 'undo' command to fix a mistake; • Can use the search tool to find the answers to simple questions; • Is able to create lists by using the return key; • Uses the shift key and capital lock for capital letters; • Successfully enters a sequence of instructions onto a floor robot.

ICT: Main Attributes of ICT, Taking Account of the Identified Bands

Stage 17: Children Identified at 2b Secure should show the following attributes:	Stage 18: Children Identified at 2b Upper should show the following attributes:
• Can alter the layout of a text to make it easier to read; • Is able to able to device questions that have a yes/no answer and can understand how a yes/no question can help to identify objects; • Knows that a database cannot answer every question; • Is able to program the floor turtle using commands forward, back, left and right; • Is able to program the turtle so that it arrives at a specific spot.	• Knows that additional fields can be added to a database; • Is able to use a pictogram to help answer specific questions; • Is able to choose colours and patterns that suit their purpose; • Is able to program a quarter, half and full turns on a floor turtle.

ICT: Main Attributes of ICT, Taking Account of the Identified Bands

Stage 19: Children Identified at 2a Secure should show the following attributes:	Stage 20: Children Identified at 2a Upper should show the following attributes:
• Can select and use simple mark making tools, for example, brush and pen tools; • Can use the spray tools; • Is able to choose colours and patterns that suit their purpose; • Is able to add an extra field to a database (unaided); • Is able to use a pictogram to help answer specific questions.	• Is able to centre and underline text; • Can change the colour, size and style of font of text; • Can use the mouse to highlight text; • Can use the shift key to produce punctuation marks such as exclamation marks.

ICT: Main Attributes of ICT, Taking Account of the Identified Bands

Stage 21: Children identified at 3c Secure should show the following attributes:	Stage 22: Children identified at 3c Upper should show the following attributes:
• Can amend text by over-typing and then save the work; • Combine text and graphics (from clip art or from CD-ROM); • Choose a font to emphasise text.	• Can compose and send e-mails; • Read and respond to e-mail; • Send an e-mail, using an address book; • Add an attachment to e-mail; • Frame appropriate questions to use for e-mail; • Prepare a message off-line to send via e-mail.

ICT: Main Attributes of ICT, Taking Account of the Identified Bands

Stage 23: Children Identified at 3b Secure should show the following attributes:	Stage 24: Children Identified at 3b Upper should show the following attributes:
• Is able to copy an e-mail message onto hard disk; • Is able to create an address book for email; • Is able to attach a sound file to an e-mail message; • Is able to gather, exchange and develop information using e-mail.	• Can enter, sort and store information in a database; • Can use a database to produce a bar chart; • Can use a database to enter simple questions; • Can use ICT to record sounds; • Can use a database to help sort and use information effectively; • Knows that a database can be searched by field.

Scrutinising Work at Key Stage One:
Science

Science:

Main Attributes of Science, Taking Account of the Identified Bands

Stage 1: Children Identified at FSP Point 1 should show the following attributes:	Stage 2: Children Identified at FSP Point 2 should show the following attributes:
• Begins to use senses to explore a variety of materials, objects and events; • Shows curiosity and interest through facial expression, movement or talk when playing with different materials and handling a variety of objects, e.g., looking through a magnifying glass, watching water flow through a water wheel, watching patterns in kaleidoscope; • Shows curiosity and interest in their natural environment, e.g. looking at minibeasts or playing with shadows.	• Can use the senses to observe and explore a variety of objects and materials; • Can describe and begin to sort living things, objects and events by different criteria, e.g., natural objects found on a walk, items from different rooms in the house, animals that live on the farm or in the wild; • Can recognise themselves in photographs, e.g., as a baby, at a birthday party.

Science:

Main Attributes of Science, Taking Account of the Identified Bands

Stage 3: Children Identified at FSP Point 3 should show the following attributes:	Stage 4: Children Identified at FSP Point 4/5 Lower should show the following attributes:
• Can identify obvious similarities and differences when exploring materials, for example recognises that metal is hard while wool is soft. They also recognise that birds and butterflies both have sets of wings; • Begins to know that certain materials are easy to join together and others are not.	• Can talk about likes and dislikes in their environment, e.g., flowers alongside a road look pretty but litter does not; • Is able to identify features of living things and talk about their personal likes and dislikes. For example, indicates that they like butterflies because of their wings; • Recognises that plants are alive and will grow if looked after properly. Recognises that pets need to be looked after carefully if they are expected to thrive.

Science:

Main Attributes of Science, Taking Account of the Identified Bands

Stage 5: Children Identified at FSP Point 4/5 Upper should show the following attributes:	Stage 6: Children Identified at FSP Point 6/7 Lower should show the following attributes:
<ul><li>Is aware of what happens if ice is left out in the sun;</li><li>Is beginning to have a growing awareness of how pushes and pulls on objects work;</li><li>Is very interested in the eating habits of different animals, such as, stick insects;</li><li>Looks at the markings on creatures, such as, caterpillars and is interested in recurring patterns, etc.;</li><li>Begins to notice changes in seasonal patterns.</li></ul>	<ul><li>Predicts what each season can bring, e.g., summer is likely to be warm; leaves fall from trees in autumn;</li><li>Can talk about how to look after a pet and what they need to help them be happy.</li></ul>

Science:

Main Attributes of Science, Taking Account of the Identified Bands

Stage 7: **Children Identified at FSP Point 6/7 Upper should show the following attributes:**	Stage 8: **Children Identified at 1c Lower (FSP Point 8 Lower) should show the following attributes:**
• Knows that the Sun disappears from the sky at approximately the same time each day; • Knows that the Sun gives light to the Earth even though it may be difficult to see the Sun because of cloud cover.	• Can show where the important parts of the body are; • Can talk about the changes that happen to humans and animals as they get older; • Names some common materials; • Knows that the Sun is an important source of light; • Knows that one cannot see in the dark.

Science:

Main Attributes of Science, Taking Account of the Identified Bands

Stage 9: Children Identified at 1c Lower (FSP Point 8 Upper) should show the following attributes:	Stage 10: Children Identified at 1c Upper (FSP Point 9 Lower) should show the following attributes:
• Can talk about the changes that happen to humans and animals as they get older; • Finds out about the characteristics of some common materials; • Knows that it is dangerous to look directly at the Sun.	• Can tell the difference between living and non-living things; • Can identify the following parts of plants: leaf, root, stem and flower; • Uses terms like, bendy, rough and hard when talking about common materials; • I know the difference between a pull and push.

Science:

Main Attributes of Science, Taking Account of the Identified Bands

Stage 11: Children Identified at 1b Secure (FSP Point 9 Upper) should show the following attributes:	Stage 12: Children Identified at 1b Upper should show the following attributes:
• Can name some common plants; • Can compare the movements made by two different objects; • Can recognise and describe different types of sounds; • Knows that I use my ears when I hear a sound.	• Is able to explain why a plant is a living thing; • Can help to make up a test about materials and say what I have found out; • Knows that it is more difficult to hear a sound when further away from the source.

Science:

Main Attributes of Science, Taking Account of the Identified Bands

Stage 13: Children Identified at 1a Secure should show the following attributes:	Stage 14: Children Identified at 1a Upper should show the following attributes:
• Knows that plants needs light and water to grow; • Can help set up an experiment to find out what a plant needs to grow; • With some help can make up a chart which shows how sound becomes softer the further away it is.	• Can talk about the difference between living and non-living objects by the way they move and grow; • Knows that living things have to be handled very carefully; • Can suggest why some materials are better for certain things than other materials; • Knows why shiny objects cannot be seen in the dark.

Science:

Main Attributes of Science, Taking Account of the Identified Bands

Stage 15: Children Identified at 2c Secure should show the following attributes:	Stage 16: Children Identified at 2c Upper should show the following attributes:
• Knows that adult animals no longer grow; • Can suggest different ways of presenting information; • Can explain what happens if a plant is not given light; • Can make predictions about outcomes when testing materials; • Knows how a water wheel or a windmill moves; • Knows that when a sound is made something moves or vibrates.	• Can name different types of food that we eat; • Knows about a balanced diet and can explain why it is important to keep healthy; • Can think of questions to help know the difference between babies and toddlers; • Can name some materials that occur naturally; • Knows how to use pushes or pulls to help an object speed up or slow down or change direction.

Science:

Main Attributes of Science, Taking Account of the Identified Bands

Stage 17: Children Identified at 2b Secure should show the following attributes:	Stage 18: Children Identified at 2b Upper should show the following attributes:
• Knows that medicine can make people better but that care needs to be taken when taking them; • Knows that animals produce babies; • Knows that heat can change materials into a different type of material; • Knows that pushes and pulls are types of forces; • Knows how to set up an experiment about the way objects move and can tell if an experiment is a fair one; • Knows a range of appliances that need electricity to make them work.	• Knows that different plants and animals live in certain places and can give examples of these; • Knows that a plant produces seeds which grow into plants; • Can describe what happens to water when it is heated or is cooled; • Knows that electricity can be dangerous and can explain why.

Science:

Main Attributes of Science, Taking Account of the Identified Bands

Stage 19: Children Identified at 2a Secure should show the following attributes:	Stage 20: Children Identified at 2a Upper should show the following attributes:
• Can record the growth of as plant on a chart and describe what was observed; • Can record observations about materials on a chart but also knows when comparisons are not fair; • Can make a drawing of a simple working electrical circuit; • Can explain why a circuit works and others may not.	• Can talk about a balanced diet; • Knows why it is sometimes necessary to take medicines; • Can describe the changes that happens to a human as they get older; • Knows that ice, steam and water are the same material and knows how to change one to another.

Science:

Main Attributes of Science, Taking Account of the Identified Bands

Stage 21: Children Identified at 3c Secure should show the following attributes:	Stage 22: Children Identified at 3c Upper should show the following attributes:
• Can explain why different plants and animals are found in different places; • Can identify the things that will not change as adults get older; • Can explain how to reverse the changes that have occurred; • Knows how to set out a circuit in a diagram and how the diagram will explain every part.	• Knows what an adequate and varied diet for humans should comprise of and knows that there are many ways of achieving one; • Knows that plants need light, water, healthy leaves, roots and stems in order to grow well; • Can tell what some common materials are used for and why they are used for certain tasks; • Can classify materials as magnetic or non-magnetic.

Science:

Main Attributes of Science, Taking Account of the Identified Bands

Stage 23: Children Identified at 3b Secure should show the following attributes:	Stage 24: Children Identified at 3b Upper should show the following attributes:
• Knows how teeth should be looked after and knows why they should be looked after; • Can set up fair experiments in order to find out more about the way plants grow; • Can describe some uses of magnets; • Knows how a shadow is formed and know that a shadow is similar in shape to the object forming it.	• Can find out information about diets and present it in many different ways; • Can set up an experiment to find out information about different materials; • Can name and tell you about the characteristics of several rocks; • Knows that a force acts in a particular direction; • Can set up an experiment to help understand what happens to shadows over a period of time.

Scrutinising Work at Key Stage One:

Design and Technology

Design and Technology:

Main Attributes of DT, Taking Account of the Identified Bands

Stage 1: Children Identified at FSP Point 1 should show the following attributes:	Stage 2: Children Identified at FSP Point 2 should show the following attributes:
• Shows curiosity when handling a variety of objects and materials; • Have an awareness of technology around them, e.g., washing machines, televisions; • Can play with and work a simple construction toy.	• Can use a range of construction materials for building simple structures; • Begins to use tools appropriately, e.g., scissors, glue spreaders and rolling pins.
Stage 3: Children Identified at FSP Point 3 should show the following attributes:	**Stage 4: Children Identified at FSP Point 4/5 Lower should show the following attributes:**
• Can make structures or models with a purpose in mind, using simple tools and techniques; • Begins to know which materials are easy to join together and which are not; • Selects the appropriate tool and equipment to carry out tasks, e.g., scissors for cutting, glue for sticking.	• Regularly uses bricks, paper, cardboard and junk to make simple constructions; • Has grown in confidence when using cutting tools such as scissors; • Is aware of the purpose of a range of tools such as scissors, blu tack, paper fasteners, velcro, etc.

Design and Technology:

Main Attributes of DT, Taking Account of the Identified Bands

Stage 5: Children Identified at FSP Point 4/5 Upper should show the following attributes:	Stage 6: Children Identified at FSP Point 6/7 Lower should show the following attributes:
• Can select a group of materials suitable for making something; • Observes detail in materials and objects.	• Can explore how things work by dismantling safe and simple objects, e.g., torches and clocks; • Is aware of how technology is used in everyday life.
Stage 7: Children Identified at FSP Point 6/7 Upper should show the following attributes:	Stage 8: Children Identified at 1c Lower (FSP Point 8 Lower) should show the following attributes:
• Can select appropriate resources and tools for building projects; • Knows how each material works and their limitations; • Is able to explain why one material may be more appropriate than another.	• Have used construction kits, chosen by their teacher; • With help, have made a moving object; • Can describe tastes and textures of some fruit and vegetables; • With support, can build a model from reclaimed materials.

Design and Technology:

Main Attributes of DT, Taking Account of the Identified Bands

Stage 9: Children Identified at 1c Secure (FSP Point 8 Upper) should show the following attributes:	Stage 10: Children Identified at 1c Upper (FSP Point 9 Lower) should show the following attributes:
• Have constructed models mainly from one type of kit following instructions or plans; • Can build a model from construction kit components and attach features to the model, e.g., roofs and windows using sheet or reclaimed materials.	• Have used tools safely to make an object that incorporates a simple lever or slider; • Have used given techniques to practise their making skills and as a starting point for developing their own ideas; • Have joined construction kit components together and combined them with other materials; • Have successfully constructed a realistic model of an item, such as playground equipment; • Have an understanding of the properties, including taste, texture and appearance, of a range of fruit and vegetables; • Can construct a model home, incorporating the main features of windows and doors.
Stage 11: Children Identified at 1b Secure (FSP Point 9 Upper) should show the following attributes:	**Stage 12: Children Identified at 1b Upper should show the following attributes:**
• Have been able to talk about how simple moving products work; • Have assembled a model with accuracy and can talk about how it is appropriate for the intended user; • Can prepare and combine ingredients into a specific product; • Shows an understanding of different types of buildings and their main features.	• Have developed their own ideas from initial starting points; • Have made simple judgements about their work; • Have used a wide range of materials and construction techniques; • Have incorporated some type of movement into their model; • Can add more details and features to a construction, e.g., stairs, interior rooms, cut-out windows, curtains, gutters and be able to say why they have included them.

Design and Technology:

Main Attributes of DT, Taking Account of the Identified Bands

Stage 13: Children Identified at 1a Secure should show the following attributes:	Stage 14: Children Identified at 1a Upper should show the following attributes:
• Have recorded their models through drawing and labelling; • Can easily identify what is, and what is not, working well with their model; • Has a basic understanding of structures to make their models strong and stable.	• Can make clear suggestions as to what they intend to do; • Can make a winding mechanism from construction kits; • With support, can use a graphics program with support.
Stage 15: Children Identified at 2c Secure should show the following attributes:	**Stage 16: Children Identified at 2c Upper should show the following attributes:**
• Can attempt to create a vehicle, which represents their original idea; • With support, can create an object such as a puppet by gluing two pieces of fabric together and added features using appropriate materials and techniques. • After prompting, will have suggested at least one improvement to their idea.	• After clarifying ideas through discussion, have gained an understanding of how simple mechanisms related to moving vehicles work; • Will have discussed their ideas as they develop and be able to say what their design has to do; • Will have gained an understanding of simple winding mechanisms and make realistic suggestions as to how their ideas can be achieved; • Can construct mechanisms using construction kits and reclaimed materials; • Can use graphics program to try out their ideas and suggest improvements.

Design and Technology:

Main Attributes of DT, Taking Account of the Identified Bands

Stage 17: Children Identified at 2b Secure should show the following attributes:	Stage 18: Children Identified at 2b Upper should show the following attributes:
• Can make a wheeled vehicle which moves and which generally matches their design intention; • will have stitched two pieces of fabric together and added features using appropriate materials and techniques; • Can say what works well in their model; • With minimal guidance, can work with increasing care and accuracy the tools and techniques shown to them.	• Shows a wider understanding of a model and will have incorporated moving parts, e.g., opening doors and windows, tipping bodies or simple steering into their design, after reflecting on their early ideas; • Can reflect on their own ideas and worked independently to create their an object like a puppet using appropriate techniques to measure, mark-out and join the fabric pieces they have selected; • When making an object such as a puppet will have added features to capture particular characteristics and expressions; • Can communicate their ideas clearly and make a model with two or more winding mechanisms; • Can use a graphics program competently to show realistic ideas.
Stage 19: Children Identified at 2a Secure should show the following attributes:	Stage 20: Children Identified at 2a Upper should show the following attributes:
• Can create a working model which, matches their design intention, after having made judgements about what they want the design to do; • Can identify how well an object such as a puppet works in relation to simple design criteria; • Can connect one mechanism to another so that one turns the other that is driven; • Can make judgements about their product in relation to their design idea and suggested improvements to their design.	• Knows that most packaging can be unfolded to form a net; • Can gather a range of ingredients needed to prepare a snack; • Will have developed a limited understanding of simple pneumatic systems; • With support can make a free standing photograph frame.

Design and Technology:

Main Attributes of DT, Taking Account of the Identified Bands

Stage 21: Children Identified at 3c Secure should show the following attributes:	**Stage 22: Children Identified at 3c Upper should show the following attributes:**
• Can use a pre-drawn net and use it to create a package; • Can prepare a snack and discuss how it meets a given purpose; • With support, can work with others to create a model with a moving part controlled by a pneumatic system.	• Will have investigated a commercially made package and recognise how they are assembled; • Can evaluate their original package against their original criteria; • Can work as part of a team to design and make at least one moving part controlled by a pneumatic system; • Can understand ways in which structures can be made more stable.
Stage 23: Children Identified at 3b Secure should show the following attributes:	**Stage 24: Children Identified at 3b Upper should show the following attributes:**
• Can make up mock-ups of their ideas before measuring, marking out, cutting and assembling with accuracy; • Can produce packaging that is visually lively, accurately made and appropriate for its purpose; • Can consider how well a snack they have designed meets its original purpose; • Will have developed an understanding of simple pneumatic systems.	• Can produce labelled diagrams of ideas to be made at a later time; • Will be able to match materials, tools and techniques to the task; • Will have identified what is and is not working well and suggest at least one modification; • Can offer suggestions for modifications to their original idea; • Will have worked as part of a team to design and make a model that has two moving parts controlled by a pneumatic system.

Scrutinising Work at Key Stage One:

History/Geography

History/Geography:

Main Attributes of History/Geography, Taking Account of the Identified Bands

Stage 1: Children Identified at FSP Point 1 should show the following attributes:	Stage 2: Children Identified at FSP Point 2 should show the following attributes:
• Can recognise familiar people and places within their daily lives, e.g., school crossing patrol person; • Begins to understand how time passes, e.g., they will eventually be older.	• Can recognise themselves in photographs, e.g., as a baby, at a birthday party; • Can recognise and name familiar features in their local environment, e.g., church, swimming baths, temple, post box, bus stop, etc.

History/Geography:

Main Attributes of History/Geography, Taking Account of the Identified Bands

Stage 3: Children Identified at FSP Point 3 should show the following attributes:	Stage 4: Children Identified at FSP Point 4/5 Lower should show the following attributes:
• Cognises words like yesterday or phrases like last year as belonging to something that has past; • Recognises similarities and differences in the environment such as looking at road signs, etc.	• Can talk about why certain buildings are needed in the locality. For example, a supermarket; • Can talk about which place they would go to buy certain materials; • Is able to recognise and name their house or street they live in from a photograph.

History/Geography:

Main Attributes of History/Geography, Taking Account of the Identified Bands

Stage 5: Children Identified at FSP Point 4/5 Upper should show the following attributes:	Stage 6: Children Identified at FSP Point 6/7 Lower should show the following attributes:
• Has an awareness of the names of shops in their locality, e.g., butcher, baker, post office; • Is able to name the largest town or city nearest to them.	• Can discuss events in terms of time such as: today; tomorrow; yesterday; last week; • Uses family photographs and video recordings to find out more about own family; • Can talk about important events in their own life, e.g., birthday, etc.

History/Geography:

Main Attributes of History/Geography, Taking Account of the Identified Bands

Stage 7: Children Identified at FSP Point 6/7 Upper should show the following attributes:	Stage 8: Children Identified at 1c Lower (FSP Point 8 Lower) should show the following attributes:
• Can sort a selection of objects into old and new; • Can find out about him/herself, and events in own life by asking questions of family members.	• Can identify the main differences between old and new objects; • Uses words and phrases like old, new and very old to help understand about the passing of time.

History/Geography:

Main Attributes of History/Geography, Taking Account of the Identified Bands

Stage 9: Children Identified at 1c Secure (FSP Point 8 Upper) should show the following attributes:	Stage 10: Children Identified at 1c Upper (FSP Point 9 Lower) should show the following attributes:
• Can ask and answer questions about old and new objects, such as toys; • Can talk about their own home explaining what can be found in different rooms.	• Begins to recognise what it means to belong to a variety of groups and communities, e.g., recognise some celebrations, customs, festivals and practices of a variety of different groups; • Recognises the distinction between present and past in their own and others people's lives.

History/Geography:

Main Attributes of History/Geography, Taking Account of the Identified Bands

Stage 11: Children Identified at 1b Secure (FSP Point 9 Upper) should show the following attributes:	Stage 12: Children Identified at 1b Upper should show the following attributes:
• Can begin to offer some explanation about the differences between old and new objects; • Recognises old household artefacts and can say in which room they would be found.	• Can begin to compare their home life now with the home life of their grandparents; • Can make up maps represent make believe places.

History/Geography:

Main Attributes of History/Geography, Taking Account of the Identified Bands

Stage 13: Children Identified at 1a Secure should show the following attributes:	Stage 14: Children Identified at 1a Upper should show the following attributes:
• Can order a set of objects correctly in chronological order; • Is aware that geographical features differ from place to place, e.g., some areas of flat while others are hilly.	• Is happy to lean about the past by talking to an older person; • Uses an increasing number of geographical terms, such as, hill; river and road when describing what they can see; • Can start to talk about contrasting localities.

History/Geography:

Main Attributes of History/Geography, Taking Account of the Identified Bands

Stage 15: Children Identified at 2c Secure should show the following attributes:	Stage 16: Children Identified at 2c Upper should show the following attributes:
• Knows that there are several ways of finding out about the past; • Knows own address; • Knows about the effects of weather on themselves and their surroundings.	• Follows directions, including terms like, front of; far; near; right; left; north; south; east and west; • Knows that they live in the UK and that the UK is made up of England, Wales, Scotland and Northern Ireland.

History/Geography:

Main Attributes of History/Geography, Taking Account of the Identified Bands

Stage 17: Children Identified at 2b Secure should show the following attributes:	Stage 18: Children Identified at 2b Upper should show the following attributes:
• Uses and makes up real and imaginary maps; • Can point to the place they live on the map of the UK; • Is able to appreciate the difference between something old and something that is worn.	• Can order a set of photographs or pictures in chronological sequence giving good reasons for their order; • Is able to follow a route on a map or plan; • Can talk about likes and dislikes in relation to the environment.

History/Geography:

Main Attributes of History/Geography, Taking Account of the Identified Bands

Stage 19: Children Identified at 2a Secure should show the following attributes:	Stage 20: Children Identified at 2a Upper should show the following attributes:
• Uses maps and globes to identify major geographical features, e.g., sea, rivers and cities; • Can use a range of information to ask and answer questions about vents in the past.	• Can appreciate the difference between a village, town and city; • Knows that people who lived in the past cooked differently, travelled differently and used different weapons to us.

History/Geography:

Main Attributes of History/Geography, Taking Account of the Identified Bands

Stage 21: Children Identified at 3c Secure should show the following attributes:	Stage 22: Children Identified at 3c Upper should show the following attributes:
• Knows that people can affect the environment for good or worse; • Recognises that people who have lived in the past will have helped to shape our lives today; • Begins to recognise that different people have differing views of events in history; • Knows of a range of artefacts used by people in the past and can explain how they work.	• Knows that different people across the world experience different weather patterns to our own; • Uses picture different sources and reconstructions to find out more about a particular period in history; • Is able to communicate knowledge and understanding orally and in writing and offer points of view based upon what they have found out; • Recognises that the lives of wealth people was very different to that of poor people.

History/Geography:

Main Attributes of History/Geography, Taking Account of the Identified Bands

Stage 23: Children Identified at 3b Secure should show the following attributes:	Stage 24: Children Identified at 3b Upper should show the following attributes:
• Knows that people living in warm climates dress differently to us and have to adapt their lives accordingly; • Recognises the main similarities and differences between a time in the past and now.	• Shows a developing ability to ask and respond to geographical questions and expresses views about physical and human features of the environment; • Shows a degree of empathy with children who used to live in the past and can recognise how their lives would be different to their own; • Describes and compares features of their local area and identifies changes within and across different periods of time.

Scrutinising Work at Key Stage One:

Physical Education

Physical Education:

Main Attributes of Physical Education, Taking Account of the Identified Bands

Stage 1: Children Identified at FSP Point 1 should show the following attributes:	Stage 2: Children Identified at FSP Point 2 should show the following attributes:
• Begins to move spontaneously using available space; • Can join in hand rhymes and action games; • Uses body movements to respond to stories; • Shows improving some control over stopping and starting in response to music; • Begins to explore different ways of moving through play, e.g., running in the outdoor play area pretending to be different things.	• Carries out a range of activities, such as, climbing, riding a bike and jumping from a height with confidence; • Incorporates imagination into movements by hanging upside down from climbing frame or pedalling backwards on bike.; • Can create movements in response to story stimuli; • Moves around the perimeter of personal space; • Moves from space to space using whole area and avoiding others.

Physical Education:

Main Attributes of Physical Education, Taking Account of the Identified Bands

Stage 3: Children Identified at FSP Point 3 should show the following attributes:	Stage 4: Children Identified at FSP Point 4/5 Lower should show the following attributes:
• Shows good control in own movements and can balance for more than 3 seconds on one leg; • Can hold a shape in a fixed position for a small time on the apparatus and floor; • Can move in a variety of directions and with different speeds with some control; • Can sit, stand, run, jump and balance on various parts of body with developing control; • Can change speed and direction effectively to avoid obstacles.	• Negotiates fixed apparatus with confidence using dominant foot to climb on and then using alternative feet to move along; • Can move off apparatus and land appropriately; • Moves with good control and co-ordination when running, jumping, skipping, sliding, hopping, rolling, balancing and climbing.

Physical Education:

Main Attributes of Physical Education, Taking Account of the Identified Bands

Stage 5: Children Identified at FSP Point 4/5 Upper should show the following attributes:	Stage 6: Children Identified at FSP Point 6/7 Lower should show the following attributes:
• Explores different ways of moving across apparatus, moving under, over, through and around as the apparatus demands; • Can change direction and speed effectively to avoid obstacles; • Shows a good variety of movements when working on the floor or on apparatus; • Can repeat a movement with a view to improving; • Shows uniqueness by moving in a way that no one else has thought of.	• Can sit and slide along a wide balancing beam; • Can crawl along a wide balancing beam; • Can walk along a wide and narrow balancing beam; • Can climb up rungs or bars on a climbing frame; • Moves under climbing frame or gym equipment by: lying down; and sliding; crawling or rolling; • Crawls through the bars on climbing frame or gym equipment; • Climbs on and over boxes, benches, etc.; • Moves around equipment using hands and feet to hold on.

Physical Education:

Main Attributes of Physical Education, Taking Account of the Identified Bands

Stage 7: Children Identified at FSP Point 6/7 Upper should show the following attributes:	Stage 8: Children Identified at 1c Lower (FSP Point 8 Lower) should show the following attributes:
• Can roll or kick a ball for up to 10 meters; • Can throw a ball or beanbag accurately over a 2 meters length; • Can throw a beanbag up to a height of 1 metre and catch it; • Can throw a ball into a net; • Can kick a ball into a goal; • Shows reasonable control when dribbling a ball; • Can hit a ball with a large bat.	• Is aware of the need to be healthy in order to work and play and to fight off germs and illnesses; • Is aware that in order to remain healthy they have to eat a balanced diet; exercise regularly; get plenty of sleep and keep themselves clean; • Knows that they need to do different things to keep healthy; • Knows that it is important for them to walk and run during playtimes; • Knows that it is not good to sit in front of the television for too long; • Is happy to join in play vigorously with others.

Physical Education:

Main Attributes of Physical Education, Taking Account of the Identified Bands

Stage 9: Children Identified at 1c Secure (FSP Point 8 Upper) should show the following attributes:	Stage 10: Children Identified at 1c Upper (FSP Point 9 Lower) should show the following attributes:
• Shows awareness of what happens to the body during and after exercise; • Knows that the body becomes hot when they have been running around and notices that their heart rate increases; • Knows that they may perspire, breathe faster, and become out of breath; • Is aware that when they are active changes will occur to the body.	• Can work out a simple movement on or off apparatus with or without music and remember it well enough to repeat it; • Repeats and changes movements and actions in order to think about, refine and improve them; • Can link, repeat and change movements and actions to think about, refine and improve them.

Physical Education:

Main Attributes of Physical Education, Taking Account of the Identified Bands

Stage 11: Children Identified at 1b Secure (FSP Point 9 Upper) should show the following attributes:	Stage 12: Children Identified at 1b Upper should show the following attributes:
• Can demonstrate good control of body when using large or small apparatus; • Can throw a small or medium sized ball up a distance of one metre and catch it with both hands; • Can work co-operatively with a partner during a range of activities, e.g., with bat and ball or when making up a dance sequence.	• Can remember and repeat short dance phrases, moving with good control; • Choose movements in dance that shows good understanding of the dance idea and takes account of the music; • Can catch a bean bag or medium sized ball thrown to them from up to 5 meters away; • Can choose different ways of hitting, throwing, striking or kicking a ball; • Can confidently make their bodies tense, relaxed, curled or stretched; • Uses words like rolling, balancing, travelling or climbing in relation to gymnastic movements.

Physical Education:

Main Attributes of Physical Education, Taking Account of the Identified Bands

Stage 13: Children Identified at 1a Secure should show the following attributes:	Stage 14: Children Identified at 1a Upper should show the following attributes:
• Can talk about their dances using appropriate language associated with their movements; • Is beginning to appreciate tactics in small games, e.g., knows where to stand to make it difficult for an opponent; • Gymnastic movements have a clear beginning, middle and end; • Describes their own and others' gymnastics movements, sometimes offering ideas about improving them.	• Can choose movements that best suit the dance idea and music; • Can describe simple tactics in small game situations; • Can tell when they have performed a gymnastic action well, showing control; • *Is confident in shallow water.*

Physical Education:

Main Attributes of Physical Education, Taking Account of the Identified Bands

Stage 15: Children Identified at 2c Secure should show the following attributes:	Stage 16: Children Identified at 2c Upper should show the following attributes:
• Can express idea, feeling and mood of intended dance phrase; • Applies skills of striking, rolling and kicking in a small game situation; • Shows awareness of team mates and opponents in a small game situation; • *With the aid of arm bands, is willing to have a go at swimming over a length of at least 5 meters.*	• Understands why it is important to warm up before dancing or performing a gymnastic movement; • Links actions with increased control in gymnastics and dance; • Can work with a partner to create a sequence; • Can use a range of tactics when playing a game.

Physical Education:

Main Attributes of Physical Education, Taking Account of the Identified Bands

Stage 17: Children Identified at 2b Secure should show the following attributes:	Stage 18: Children Identified at 2b Upper should show the following attributes:
• With a partner, can create, repeat and improve a sequence showing at least 3 phases; • Can kick a ball accurately to a partner or a point over a distance of 10 meters; • Can change their body shape by linking movements during a gymnastic movement; • *Swims unaided over a distance of 10 meters.*	• Can dance imaginatively, changing rhythm, speed, level and direction of their movements; • Can travel with, send and receive a ball or other equipment in different ways; • In gymnastics, can perform movements with skill and safety showing good awareness of space and partner's needs.

Physical Education:

Main Attributes of Physical Education, Taking Account of the Identified Bands

Stage 19: Children Identified at 2a Secure should show the following attributes:	Stage 20: Children Identified at 2a Upper should show the following attributes:
• Can create and perform dances using more complex movement patterns, including those from different times and cultures; • Participates with eagerness in small sided games showing good tactics from both an attacking and defensive point of view; • In gymnastics, can create and perform short, linked sequences that have clear beginnings, middle and ends showing contrasts in direction, level and speed.	• Creates dance phrase by self, with partner or in a small group that can communicate ideas; • Can move to find space when they are not in possession during a ball game; • Can balance on different parts of the body on two or three points showing good control.

Physical Education:

Main Attributes of Physical Education, Taking Account of the Identified Bands

Stage 21: Children Identified at 3c Secure should show the following attributes:	Stage 22: Children Identified at 3c Upper should show the following attributes:
• Knows why it is important to warm up and cool down; • Shows good level of improvisation when developing a dance idea; • Passes a ball with increased accuracy to a partner on their own side; • Recognises how suppleness and strength affect the quality of the performance.	• Uses dynamic, rhythmic and expressive qualities clearly and with control; • Knows and uses rules fairly to keep games going; • Can collect, stop and intercept a ball with increasing accuracy.

Physical Education:

Main Attributes of Physical Education, Taking Account of the Identified Bands

Stage 23: Children Identified at 3b Secure should show the following attributes:	Stage 24: Children Identified at 3b Upper should show the following attributes:
• Can suggest improvements to their own and others' dances; • Keeps possession with some success in ball games; • Can make up own small sided games and understands the point of the game.	• Takes the lead when creating dances with a partner or a group; • Decides quickly where and when to pass a ball so as to keep possession showing good awareness of what is happening around them; • Can vary tactics and adapt skills according to what is happening within a game; • Can change the pace, length and direction of their throws and shots, to outwit opponents.

Scrutinising Work at Key Stage One:
Art

Art: Main Attributes of Art, Taking Account of the Identified Bands

Stage 1: Children Identified at FSP Point 1 should show the following attributes:	Stage 2: Children Identified at FSP Point 2 should show the following attributes:
• Can recognise and name six colours, usually including red, white, black, blue, yellow and green; • Enjoys using a variety of media, e.g., paint, glue, collage, etc.	• Starts to make simple representations in painting, collage and model making; • Experiments with colour mixing noting changes in the colour; • Can hold a pencil in different ways to create different effects.
Stage 3: Children Identified at FSP Point 3 should show the following attributes:	Stage 4: Children Identified at FSP Point 4/5 Lower should show the following attributes:
• Chooses particular colours in their creative work to use for a purpose, e.g., choosing to use the red paint; • Begins to use shapes and patterns in different art media to represent simple figures and objects.	• With support, can mix own paint colours; • Self-portraits include features such as, fingers, hair, texture of clothes.

Art: Main Attributes of Art, Taking Account of the Identified Bands

Stage 5: Children Identified at FSP Point 4/5 Upper should show the following attributes:	Stage 6: Children Identified at FSP Point 6/7 Lower should show the following attributes:
• Is able to make simple representations with simple shapes; • Can make simple repetitive patterns with pencil or paint.	• Knows the likely outcome when two colours of paint are mixed together; • Knows that different drawing tools make different marks.
Stage 7: Children Identified at FSP Point 6/7 Upper should show the following attributes:	**Stage 8: Children Identified at 1c Lower (FSP Point 8 Lower) should show the following attributes:**
• Knows how to make a darker or lighter shade of any given colour by adding white or black accordingly.	• Can create moods in drawings and paintings; • When model making is able to distinguish between different materials so that it is easier for them to be successful.

Art: Main Attributes of Art, Taking Account of the Identified Bands

Stage 9: Children Identified at 1c Secure (FSP Point 8 Upper) should show the following attributes:	Stage 10: Children Identified at 1c Upper (FSP Point 9 Lower) should show the following attributes:
• When colouring in they do so carefully inside lines and evenly; • Is able to evaluate their model and add or amend the model accordingly; • Can talk about what they feel about their work.	• Uses more than one drawing tool to create the right effect; • Uses drawings and paintings to communicate ideas about themselves; • Can explain why they prefer certain pieces of art work
Stage 11: Children Identified at 1b Secure (FSP Point 9 Upper) should show the following attributes:	**Stage 12: Children Identified at 1b Upper should show the following attributes:**
• Responds to own work and that of others when exploring and communicating ideas, feelings and preferences through art; • Can talk about the differences between two pieces of art work; • Can continue to suggest ways of improving own work.	• Their self portraits give a good indication as to what they feel about themselves; • Can adapt and improve their own work.

Art: Main Attributes of Art, Taking Account of the Identified Bands

Stage 13: Children Identified at 1a Secure should show the following attributes:	Stage 14: Children Identified at 1a Upper should show the following attributes:
• Can use a range of repeated patterns to create desired effect; • Explores and uses man made and natural materials to communicate ideas through collage.	• Recognises the difference when using a hard or soft pencil or thick or thin brushes; • Creates different tones by using dark and light; • Explores ideas about sculptures.
Stage 15: Children Identified at 2c Secure should show the following attributes:	**Stage 16: Children Identified at 2c Upper should show the following attributes:**
• Chooses the most appropriate pencil or brush to use when drawing or painting; • Uses a view finder to focus on a specific part of an artefact before drawing it.	• Uses ideas and processes to communicate ideas in 3D; • Regularly considers the use of one of three grades of pencil when drawing, e.g., 4B, HB or 4H.

Art: Main Attributes of Art, Taking Account of the Identified Bands

Stage 17: Children Identified at 2b Secure should show the following attributes:	Stage 18: Children Identified at 2b Upper should show the following attributes:
• Investigates shape, pattern and texture; • Makes up prints based on patterns in the environment.	• Can draw imaginatively and from memory; • Can observe carefully and then record their perceptions of what they have seen; • Investigates shape, form and texture in materials to create 3D form.
Stage 19: Children Identified at 2a Secure should show the following attributes:	Stage 20: Children Identified at 2a Upper should show the following attributes:
• Begins to appreciate the impact of light and dark on simple objects; • Can organise own working area and clear up effectively afterwards.	• Records first hand observations using a range of appropriate materials; • Can cope with overlapping shapes in drawing.

Art: Main Attributes of Art, Taking Account of the Identified Bands

Stage 21: Children Identified at 3c Secure should show the following attributes:	Stage 22: Children Identified at 3c Upper should show the following attributes:
• Selects and records visual and other information in a sketchbook; • Makes informed choices because of the experience they have with a range of media.	• Uses ideas from own sketchbook to create and develop their own ideas; • Explores the application of wet/dry paint.
Stage 23: Children Identified at 3b Secure should show the following attributes:	Stage 24: Children Identified at 3b Upper should show the following attributes:
• Has extensive ability to look carefully and consider shape, tone and texture and drawings and paintings; • Chooses from a range of media the most appropriate way of communicating their ideas and experiences; • Work reflects mood and emotion as well as visual representation.	• Explores how shape and colour can be organised and combined to create patterns for different purposes; • Collects and records visual and other information about a specific location.

Scrutinising Work at Key Stage One:

Music

Music: Main Attributes of Music, Taking Account of the Identified Bands

Stage 1: Children Identified at FSP Point 1 should show the following attributes:	Stage 2: Children Identified at FSP Point 2 should show the following attributes:
• Knows the difference between singing and speaking; • Responds to music by tapping or humming.	• Knows some familiar songs/rhymes and has some understanding of simple rhymes; • Begins to respond imaginatively to music through movement.
Stage 3: Children Identified at FSP Point 3 should show the following attributes:	Stage 4: Children Identified at FSP Point 4/5 Lower should show the following attributes:
• Listens and responds to different types of music and sounds and recognises sound changes, e.g., loud/quiet/slow fast; • Chooses from a selection of instruments to accompany music and songs.	• Hums a favourite pop or popular song; • Can sing the chorus of these songs from memory; • Has a repertoire of simple songs which they can sing from memory.

Music: Main Attributes of Music, Taking Account of the Identified Bands

Stage 5: Children Identified at FSP Point 4/5 Upper should show the following attributes:	Stage 6: Children Identified at FSP Point 6/7 Lower should show the following attributes:
• Can perform songs as a class group or individually; • Readily joins in with these class singing situations.	• Begins to identify and repeat sounds and simple patterns, using percussion, voice and hands; • Responds to different moods in music orally and through movement; • Can choose instruments to represent different sounds, e.g., bells for rain; • Begins to create simple repeated rhythms.
Stage 7: Children Identified at FSP Point 6/7 Upper should show the following attributes:	Stage 8: Children Identified at 1c Lower (FSP Point 8 Lower) should show the following attributes:
• Can talk about feelings evoked by a piece of music or dance; • Begins to create their own music and songs to accompany their play; • Recognise and explore how sounds can be changed; • Enters into given role in response to story, piece of music and can develop this imaginatively.	• Recognise and explore how sounds can be changed; • Enter into given role in response to story or piece of music and can develop this imaginatively.

MUSIC: Main Attributes of Music, Taking Account of the Identified Bands

Stage 9: Children Identified at 1c Secure (FSP Point 8 Upper) should show the following attributes:	Stage 10: Children Identified at 1c Upper (FSP Point 9 Lower) should show the following attributes:
• Can talk about feelings evoked by a piece of music or dance; • Enjoys singing either individually or as part of a large group.	• Can recognise that different musical instruments creates different moods and feelings; • Can explain why they prefer certain types of music.
Stage 11: Children Identified at 1b Secure (FSP Point 9 Upper) should show the following attributes:	**Stage 12: Children Identified at 1b Upper should show the following attributes:**
• Listens carefully and recalls short rhythmic and melodic patterns; • Responds to own work and that of others when exploring and communicating ideas, feelings and preferences through music; • Can talk about the differences between two pieces of music.	• Uses voice expressively by singing songs and speaking chants; • Responds to different moods in music and recognises well-defined changes in sounds.

MUSIC: Main Attributes of Music, Taking Account of the Identified Bands

Stage 13: Children Identified at 1a Secure should show the following attributes:	Stage 14: Children Identified at 1a Upper should show the following attributes:
• Can identify simple repeated patterns and take account of musical introductions; • Can rehearse and perform with others; • Recognises that own voice can be used in different ways.	• Sings simple songs from memory with enjoyment; • Uses voice confidently in a variety of ways; • Listens carefully and recalls short rhythmic and melodic patterns.
Stage 15: Children Identified at 2c Secure should show the following attributes:	Stage 16: Children Identified at 2c Upper should show the following attributes:
• Identifies different ways sounds can be made and changed; • Recognises and responds to changes in tempo (speed of pulse).	• Shows physical control when playing musical instruments; • Repeats and creates short rhythmic phrases confidently.

MUSIC: Main Attributes of Music, Taking Account of the Identified Bands

Stage 17: Children Identified at 2b Secure should show the following attributes:	Stage 18: Children Identified at 2b Upper should show the following attributes:
• Sings simple songs accurately at a given pitch and with clear diction and expression. • Recognises and explores how sounds can be organised.	• Identifies subtle changes in sounds and recalls complete phrases. • Makes controlled long and short sounds using voice and instruments.
Stage 19: Children Identified at 2a Secure should show the following attributes:	**Stage 20: Children Identified at 2a Upper should show the following attributes:**
• Shows considerable physical control of instruments and of their bodies when performing and responding to music; • Carefully chooses sounds and instruments and suggests how they should be used and played; • Works in partnership with a friend to create a sequence of long and short sounds.	• Sings songs from memory with accuracy of pitch, in a group or alone; • Works with a small group to compose, perform and record extended sequences involving sounds of varying duration.

MUSIC: Main Attributes of Music, Taking Account of the Identified Bands

Stage 21: Children Identified at 3c Secure should show the following attributes:	Stage 22: Children Identified at 3c Upper should show the following attributes:
• Understands the importance of articulating the words to communicate the song to an audience; • Is able to direct the work of others.	• Demonstrates increasing aural memory and physical control; • Creates descriptive music, e.g., based on animals, that uses a sequence of sounds.
Stage 23: Children Identified at 3b Secure should show the following attributes:	**Stage 24: Children Identified at 3b Upper should show the following attributes:**
• Practices, rehearses and presents performances with an awareness of the audience; • Suggests ways of improving performance of a song; • Identifies subtle changes and differences.	• Sings songs, in unison and two parts, with clear diction, control of pitch, a sense of phrase and musical expression; • Will work in groups of three or four to extend their ideas in to longer pieces of music with several layers of sounds.

Scrutinising Work at Key Stage One:

Personal, Social & Health Education

Personal, Social & Health Education:

Main Attributes of PSHCE, Taking Account of the Identified Bands

Stage 1: Children Identified at FSP Point 1 should show the following attributes:	Stage 2: Children Identified at FSP Point 2 should show the following attributes:
• Tends to watch and listen before joining in; • Begins to communicate with familiar friends; • Can communicate needs to familiar adults; • Is happy to use the same materials or resources as others; • Tends to identify with one prominent adult.	• Attempts to dress and undress for PE and dance; • Will wash hands after using toilet; • Tends to communicate with others through single words or short phrases; • Plays alongside others after watching what is happening first. • Feels part of the class; • Is able to follow familiar routines.
Stage 3: Children Identified at FSP Point 3 should show the following attributes:	**Stage 4: Children Identified at FSP Point 4/5 Lower should show the following attributes:**
• Will concentrate for a lengthy period on a given activity; • Will often return to an activity after a break; • Takes part in make-believe or imaginative play; • Will sometimes make first moves to join in with others; • Can talk to someone about being happy or sad.	• Will help with pouring drinks at snack time; • Is very independent when dressing and undressing; • Will share equipment with others; • Shows patience when waiting turn; • Shows excitement when doing an activity they like.

Personal, Social & Health Education:

Main Attributes of PSHCE, Taking Account of the Identified Bands

Stage 5: Children Identified at FSP Point 4/5 Upper should show the following attributes:	Stage 6: Children Identified at FSP Point 6/7 Lower should show the following attributes:
• Selects own resources when working independently; • Is happy to select own resources from a given selection; • Is happy to talk to adults who are at school for short periods, e.g. lunchtime supervisors; • Often uses 'please' and 'thank you'; • Shows an interest in what others have to say; • Can recognise if their friend is feeling sad.	• Is patient when listening to others talk about their ideas; • Is a good listener and will carry on with an activity even if s/he finds it difficult; • Knows what is and is not acceptable behaviour; • Is happy to take directions from adults; • Knows that other cultures have different types of celebrations.
Stage 7: Children Identified at FSP Point 6/7 Upper should show the following attributes:	**Stage 8: Children Identified at 1c Lower (FSP Point 8 Lower) should show the following attributes:**
• Will try out new ideas on own; • Will initiate ideas when working with a group; • Has an awareness that there are many special days celebrated by different groups of people; • Recognises the consequences of being selfish; • Is sensitive to the feelings of others when talking in a small or large group.	• Will sit attentively for prolonged periods, as in assembly; • Is aware that their own beliefs and ideas matter; • Understands that they have right to be treated fairly; • Knows the difference between right and wrong; • Can value the property of others

Personal, Social & Health Education:

Main Attributes of PSHCE, Taking Account of the Identified Bands

Stage 9: Children Identified at 1c Secure (FSP Point 8 Upper) should show the following attributes:	Stage 10: Children Identified at 1c Upper (FSP Point 9 Lower) should show the following attributes:
• Can listen to instructions and carry them out without being distracted; • Very rarely fidgets or causes minor distraction; • Is proud of own culture but is respectful of others' cultures; • Has a good self-esteem; • Can recognise if they have done something inappropriate and knows why; • Is able to explain to others why something may have been inappropriate.	• Often offers a range of ideas or solution to problems; • Is motivated enough to' get on' with work on own; • Works collaboratively and really listens to others' ideas; • Can follow someone else's rules and ideas; • Likes the idea of belonging to a group; • Knows that groups have to follow rules.
Stage 11: Children Identified at 1b Secure (FSP Point 9 Upper) should show the following attributes:	Stage 12: Children Identified at 1b Upper should show the following attributes:
• Settles quickly to tasks; • Is highly motivated and enjoys working; • Is happy to change own ideas if others come up with good ideas; • Can negotiate rules with others; • Is able to express likes and dislikes and knows that they may be different to the likes and dislikes of others; • Is able to express things in a caring way.	• Listens to others during circle time; • Can answer a direct question about a problem or issue related to the class; • Can make decisions after considering a limited number of options; • Identifies likes and dislikes; • Identifies what is right and wrong.

Personal, Social & Health Education:

Main Attributes of PSHCE, Taking Account of the Identified Bands

Stage 13: Children Identified at 1a Secure should show the following attributes:	Stage 14: Children Identified at 1a Upper should show the following attributes:
• Makes sensible decisions about eating healthily; • Is aware that there can be external pressures on their decision making; • Realises that they usually have several alternatives when making decisions; • Knows that animals have needs just like humans; • Knows that animals need food, water and companionship.	• Recognises that certain action can make others feel unsafe; • Eagerly participates in physical activities; • Knows that animals need a place to live; • Knows that humans need to look after animals properly; • Recognises that there are community police officers; • Knows about other members of the community that help us.
Stage 15: Children Identified at 2c Secure should show the following attributes:	Stage 16: Children Identified at 2c Upper should show the following attributes:
• Knows why it is important to drink water regularly; • Recognise the need to respect own and others' dignity; • Knows that animals need to be looked after by a vet if they are ill; • Can give examples of what the police do; • Can identify the main parts of a police uniform.	• Forms excellent relationships with everyone around them; • Uses their initiative when needed; • Knows how to ask for help in an emergency; • Knows that animals need the freedom to behave naturally.

Personal, Social & Health Education:

Main Attributes of PSHCE, Taking Account of the Identified Bands

Stage 17: Children Identified at 2b Secure should show the following attributes:	Stage 18: Children Identified at 2b Upper should show the following attributes:
• Is aware of peer and media pressure on certain circumstances; • Knows about their responsibility to keep themselves and their property safe; • Begins to appreciate that humans have responsibility to all animals – wild animals, farm animals and pets.	• Co-operates with friends and with members of staff; • Knows who to go to if feeling under pressure; • Expresses views with confidence during class discussions; • Identifies the wild life in the local area.
Stage 19: Children Identified at 2a Secure should show the following attributes:	Stage 20: Children Identified at 2a Upper should show the following attributes:
• Is very good at assessing risk and taking appropriate action; • Is particularly good at listening to the views of others and responding sensitively; • Offers simple ideas or opinions about a real school or class issue; • Knows how to help and protect wild animals.	• Leads a discussion in a simple but effective way; • Makes reasoned decisions built on sensible outcomes; • Justifies choices and can explain them to others.

Personal, Social & Health Education:

Main Attributes of PSHCE, Taking Account of the Identified Bands

Stage 21: Children Identified at 3c Secure should show the following attributes:	Stage 22: Children Identified at 3c Upper should show the following attributes:
• Copes with increasing number of alternatives when making decisions; • Can recognise that there are times when the decision taken may have been the wrong one.	• Manages changes very well and recognises that they are inevitable in some circumstances; • Understands they have responsibilities for other people; • Understands they have responsibilities for the environment.
Stage 23: Children Identified at 3b Secure should show the following attributes:	**Stage 24: Children Identified at 3b Upper should show the following attributes:**
• Will always respond sensibly to a difficult situation; • Can be relied upon to talk to a friend who is feeling low; • Justifies their decisions and can explain them; • Evaluates the consequences of their decisions.	• Can explain why certain foods are healthy and some are not; • Investigates their options through research and questioning.